W9-AEJ-586

disc

My Path to Math

123456789

Decimals

$1.02
$0.12
$4
$3.06
$8.8
$5.45
$1.1
$2.50
$2.50
$5.59
3.0

Claire Piddock

Crabtree Publishing Company
www.crabtreebooks.com

Author: Claire Piddock
Publishing plan research and development:
Sean Charlebois, Reagan Miller
Crabtree Publishing Company
Editor: Reagan Miller
Proofreader: Crystal Sikkens
Editorial director: Kathy Middleton
Project coordinator: Margaret Salter
Prepress technician: Margaret Salter
Coordinating editor: Chester Fisher
Series editor: Jessica Cohn
Project manager: Kumar Kunal (Q2AMEDIA)
Art direction: Cheena Yadav (Q2AMEDIA)
Cover design: Jasmeen Kaur (Q2AMEDIA)
Design: Kanika Kohli (Q2AMEDIA)
Photo research: Anju Pathak and Nivisha Sinha (Q2AMEDIA)
Coloring Artist: Rohit Sharma

Photographs:
Bigstockphoto: Carl Hebert: p. 7 (bottom)
Dreamstime: p. 1, 4 (left), 5, 7, 9, 17, 18, 19, 21; Tihis: p. 5; Craig Wactor:
p. 6 (pennies); Simon Howden: p. 9; Richie Lomba: p. 17 (top);
Mitja Mladkovic: p. 21 (bottom left); Dave Mcnaught: p. 9
Fotolia: Alison Bowden: p. 20 (bottom left)
Istockphoto: Augustine Chang: p. 5; Dawn Liljenquist: p. 5;
Matthew Heinrichs: p. 6 (dimes); John Burwell: p. 10, 23;
Skip Odonnell: p. 21 (top center); Maxstockphoto: p. 21 (top right)
Photos.com: p. 11, 13
Q2A Media: p. 3, 4, 5, 6, 8, 9, 10, 12, 14, 16, 18, 20, 22, 24
Other images by Shutterstock

Library and Archives Canada Cataloguing in Publication

Piddock, Claire
Decimals / Claire Piddock.

(My path to math)
Includes index.
ISBN 978-0-7787-6781-7 (bound).--ISBN 978-0-7787-6790-9 (pbk.)

1. Decimal fractions--Juvenile literature. I. Title. II. Series:
My path to math

QA117.P53 2010   j513.2'65   C2010-900974-6

Library of Congress Cataloging-in-Publication Data

Piddock, Claire.
Decimals / Claire Piddock.
p. cm. -- (My path to math)
Includes index.
ISBN 978-0-7787-6781-7 (reinforced lib. bdg. : alk. paper) -- ISBN 978-0-7787-6790-9 (pbk. : alk. paper)
1. Decimal fractions--Juvenile literature. I. Title. II. Series.

QA242.P52 2011
513.2'65--dc22

2010004411

Crabtree Publishing Company

Printed in China/072010/AP20100226

www.crabtreebooks.com   1-800-387-7650

Copyright © **2011 CRABTREE PUBLISHING COMPANY**. All rights reserved. No part of this publication may be reproduced, stored in a retrieval system or be transmitted in any form or by any means, electronic, mechanical, photocopying, recording, or otherwise, without the prior written permission of Crabtree Publishing Company.

Published in Canada
Crabtree Publishing
616 Welland Ave.
St. Catharines, ON
L2M 5V6

Published in the United States
Crabtree Publishing
PMB 59051
350 Fifth Avenue, 59th Floor
New York, New York 10118

Published in the United Kingdom
Crabtree Publishing
Maritime House
Basin Road North, Hove
BN41 1WR

Published in Australia
Crabtree Publishing
386 Mt. Alexander Rd.
Ascot Vale (Melbourne)
VIC 3032

R0430447888

Contents

At the Pet Store

Luis and his dad are shopping at a pet store. Luis has saved money. He wants to buy a toy for his pet bird.

Dad explains that the price tags show **decimal numbers**. The dot is a **decimal point**.

Numbers to the left of the decimal point have **whole number** values. They show the number of **dollars**. Numbers to the right of the decimal point have values less than one. On a price tag, these numbers show the number of **cents**.

$ 8 . 00
$ 0 . 80

dollar sign   decimal point

Luis sees a birdbath that costs 8 dollars. A bird mirror costs 80 cents.

$ 80.00

Activity Box

Read aloud the price of the canary.

Luis's dad explains how to read prices.

birdbath
$ 8.00

bird mirror
$ 0.80

Dollars and Cents

Luis counted his money before shopping.
He sorted his coins to count them.

Sorting coins is fun. One dime equals ten cents.
It takes ten dimes to make one dollar. In other
words, one dime is one-**tenth** of a dollar.
It takes 100 pennies to make one dollar.
A penny is one-**hundredth** of a dollar.

a dollar bill   10 dimes   100 pennies

Luis has five dollars. His dad teaches him how
to read price tags so Luis knows what he can
buy. In a price, each **digit** has a **place value**.
A price is like a place-value chart.

Activity Box

Which of the following
means 10 dollars and
40 cents?

$ 1.40
$10.04
$10.40
$10.00

◄ Say "and" for
the decimal point.

The 2 is in the hundreds place. The 5 is in the tens place. The 6 is in the ones place. This parrot costs "two hundred fifty-six dollars."

$ 256.00

Place-value chart

hundreds	tens	ones
2	5	6

The 2 means there are 2 sets of a hundred.

The 5 means there are 5 sets of ten.

The 6 means there are 6 ones.

Place value in the price

hundreds	tens	ones
2	5	6

The value of the 2 is $200.

The value of the 5 is $50.

The value of the 6 is $6.

Decimal Values

Luis finds a bird ladder for $2.56. He reads the price like a place-value chart. There is a 2 in the dollars place. He reads the decimal point as "and." There is a 5 in the dimes place. There is a 6 in the pennies place. It is "two dollars and fifty-six cents."

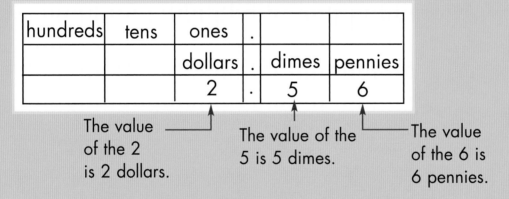

hundreds	tens	ones	.		
		dollars	.	dimes	pennies
		2	.	5	6

The value of the 2 is 2 dollars.

The value of the 5 is 5 dimes.

The value of the 6 is 6 pennies.

They see a rope perch. It is $8.06, or "eight dollars and six cents." Dad explains that the zero is a placeholder. The zero shows that there are no dimes. A price of $8.06 is not the same as $8.60!

dollars	.	dimes	pennies
8	.	0	6

Read aloud the prices
of these items.

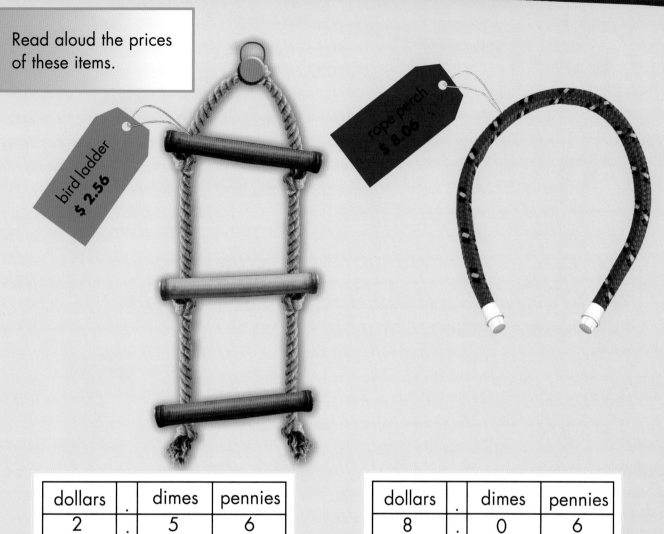

bird ladder
$ 2.56

rope perch
$ 8.06

dollars	.	dimes	pennies
2	.	5	6

dollars	.	dimes	pennies
8	.	0	6

bird feeder
$ 7.00

bird toy
$ 0.70

dollars	.	dimes	pennies
7	.	0	0

dollars	.	dimes	pennies
0	.	7	0

Tenths

Luis and his dad look at the fish, too. The fish tank has a small tool that shows the numbers 24.7°C and 76.5°F. Luis asks what these decimal numbers mean.

Dad says the numbers show the water temperature. The little circles stand for **degrees**. The C and F show two ways to measure degrees.

We measure temperature by whole degrees and parts of degrees. Whole numbers are to the left of the decimal. The first digit to the right of the decimal tells the number of tenths.

The 24.7° is "twenty-four and seven-tenths degrees." The 76.5° is "seventy-six and five-tenths degrees."

Place-value chart Degrees F (Fahrenheit)				
hundreds	tens	ones	.	tenths
	7	6	.	5

Place-value chart Degrees C (Celsius)				
hundreds	tens	ones	.	tenths
	2	4	.	7

Tenths are important when reading water temperature.

76.5°F

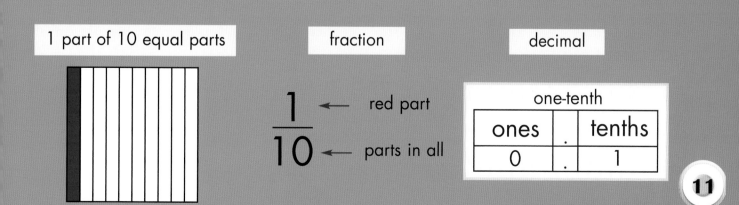

1 part of 10 equal parts	fraction	decimal

$$\frac{1}{10}$$ ← red part

← parts in all

one-tenth

ones	.	tenths
0	.	1

Hundredths

The tins of fish food have decimal numbers, too. The numbers show how much the food weighs.

Luis sees this number on a tin: 7.06

That number has two digits to the right of the decimal point! He is not sure how to read this number.

Dad says that the place to the right of the tenths is the hundredths. He says, "That number is seven and six-hundredths."

◀ The tin has 7.06 ounces of food. That is the same as 200.15 grams, or two hundred and fifteen-hundredths grams.

Activity Box

Picture hundredths as equal parts in a square. There are one hundred equal parts in a large square. Each part is a hundredth. The decimal 0.01 means "one-hundredth."

What is the decimal number for "one and one-hundredth"?

Decimals help us talk about hundreds and hundredths of things.

One part of 100 equal parts

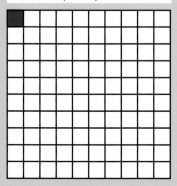

fraction

$$\frac{1}{100}$$

← red part

← parts in all

decimal

one-hundredth			
ones	.	tenths	hundredths
0	.	0	1

More Decimals

One fish tank is **half** full of water. Dad says that the **fraction** for one-half is $\frac{1}{2}$. It means "one of two equal parts."

We can show the same thing with tenths. There are ten marks on the tank's side. Each mark shows a tenth of the tank. The tank is filled to the fifth mark.

$$\frac{1}{2} = \frac{5}{10} = 0.5$$

The same tank could have 100 marks. Each could show a hundredth of the tank. The fraction could show hundredths. The decimal could show hundredths, too.

$$\frac{1}{2} = \frac{5}{10} = 0.5 = \frac{50}{100} = 0.50$$

Activity Box

Look at the boxes on the next page. Which shows one-half in tenths? Which shows one-half in hundredths?

Five out of ten fish are circled.
How can we show this as a decimal?

Compare Decimals

Tenths and hundredths are used to **compare** prices, too. Dad and Luis look at the things sold for fish tanks. They find a castle for $2.97 and rocks for $2.79. Luis lines up these prices in a place-value chart. Then he compares the digits from left to right.

He starts with the ones.
Then he goes to the tenths.

ones	.	tenths	hundredths
2	.	9	7
2	.	7	9

In other words, he compares dollars first.
Then he compares dimes. Dimes are tenths of a dollar.

Luis sees that both numbers have 2s in the ones place. He looks at tenths next. The 9 is **greater than** the 7. This means $2.97 is greater than $2.79. The castle costs more than the rocks.

Activity Box

Which one shows the price of the castle?

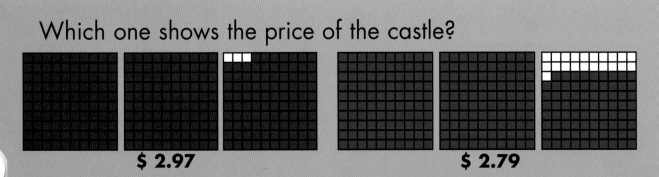

$ 2.97 $ 2.79

$ 2.97

$ 2.79

The symbol > means greater than.
The symbol < means **less than**.
$2.97 > $2.79

Order Decimals

Luis wonders how to compare more than two decimals. To explain, Dad shows three prices. He tells Luis to compare digits from left to right. Luis starts with the dollars, which are the whole numbers. Then he looks at dimes, which are tenths of a dollar. Then he goes to pennies, which are hundredths of a dollar.

Compare the ones, or dollars.

4 > 3 so $4.34 is the greatest

Then compare the tenths, or dimes.

ones	.	tenths	hundredths
4	.	3	4
3	.	3	8
3	.	2	8

3 > 2, so $3.38 > $3.28

4 > 3, so 4.34 is the greatest

3 > 2, so 3.28 is the least

The prices in order from greatest to least are $4.34, $3.38, $3.28.

Compare dollars, then dimes, and then pennies.
Find out which price is least and which is greatest.

Decimals in Your World

Luis has learned all about decimals at the pet store!

Decimals are useful. They show prices. Decimals show temperature and weight, too.

Can you use decimals? Which is reasonable for a slice of pizza?

900 cents $90.00   9 cents $0.99

Which of these can you buy with 1 dollar?

$1.10 $0.91 $0.67

Activity Box

Look for decimal numbers in newspapers, on food boxes, and elsewhere. Read the numbers aloud. See how many different ways decimals are used in the world around you.

dollars	.	dimes	pennies
ones	.	tenths	hundredths
1	.	7	5

$ 1.75

40.50 KM

MILE 1.15

ones → 1.15

↑ tenths ↑ hundredths

hundreds	tens	ones	.	tenths	hundredths
		1	.	1	5

Glossary

cents Values used for U.S. and Canadian coins; each cent stands for one-hundredth of a dollar

compare To show how one value or thing relates to another

decimal numbers Numbers written with one or more numbers to the right of a decimal point

decimal point Dot that separates numbers greater than 1 from numbers less than 1

degrees Units of measurement used in temperature

digit Any of the symbols 0, 1, 2, 3, 4, 5, 6, 7, 8, and 9

dollars Paper or coin money; each dollar has a value of 100 cents in U.S. or Canadian money

dollar sign ($) Symbol that is written to show dollar amounts in money

fraction Number that explains which part of a set or part of a whole is being used or looked at, such as $\frac{1}{4}$

greater than (>) Symbol showing which of two values is greater

half One of two equal parts

hundredth One or more of one hundred equal parts

less than (<) Symbol showing which of two values is less

place value Value assigned to each digit in a number, based on its location in the number

tenth One or more of ten equal parts

whole number One of the numbers 0, 1, 2, 3, and so on

Degrees of Difference

(F) stands for Fahrenheit
This is a temperature scale often used to describe U.S. weather.

(C) stands for Celsius This is a temperature scale used for science around the world.

Index